牙买加诗歌集萃(中英对照)

侯 涛 编译

Poems from Jamaica

山西出版传媒集团
山西人民出版社

图书在版编目（CIP）数据

牙买加诗歌集萃／侯涛编译．—太原：山西人民出版社，2020.3
ISBN 978-7-203-11261-7

Ⅰ.①牙… Ⅱ.①侯… Ⅲ.①诗集-牙买加-现代
Ⅳ.①I754.25

中国版本图书馆CIP数据核字（2020）第027812号

牙买加诗歌集萃

编　　译：侯　涛
责任编辑：任秀芳
复　　审：傅晓红
终　　审：孔庆萍
装帧设计：陈　婷

出 版 者：	山西出版传媒集团·山西人民出版社
地　　址：	太原市建设南路21号
邮　　编：	030012
发行营销：	0351-4922220　4955996　4956039　4922127（传真）
天猫官网：	https://sxrmcbs.tmall.com　电话：0351-4922159
E — mail：	sxskcb@163.com　发行部
	sxskcb@126.com　总编室
网　　址：	www.sxskcb.com

经 销 者：山西出版传媒集团·山西人民出版社
承 印 厂：山西出版传媒集团·山西新华印业有限公司

开　本：787mm×1092mm　1/16
印　张：9
字　数：100千字
印　数：1—2000册
版　次：2020年3月　第1版
印　次：2020年3月　第1次印刷
书　号：ISBN 978-7-203-11261-7
定　价：38.00元

如有印装质量问题请与本社联系调换

序　言

　　我与侯涛教授的结识还是在几年前的"北京大学——淡江大学两岸文学语言学教学研讨会"上，她当时作为代表团两位北大之外的特邀专家之一参加了那届论坛。侯涛教授温文尔雅、学养深厚，谦虚好学、思维敏捷，待人接物诚恳大方，赢得了两岸同行的一致赞誉并给我留下了深刻的印象。侯涛教授不仅是一位在语言学多个领域具有造诣，博学善导，文理、外语兼修，深受文学艺术熏陶的学者，更难能可贵的是她作为学院负责人之一，对外语学科发展有着深刻的思考和积极的担当意识。

　　转眼四年过去了，当我初次打开这本《牙买加诗歌集萃》时，我是多么地诧异！作为语言学的教授，侯涛竟将远隔大洋的西印度群岛之国牙买加全新的、包含多语种的文学作品用中文演绎得如此精妙细腻——实难想象，编译者在繁忙的教学和管理工作之余，是怎样如此出色地完成了这一弥补国内空白、意义举足轻重的翻译工作的。

　　诗歌是文学王冠上的明珠，精敛文学之魂魄，很多人都认为诗歌是不可译的。然而读罢侯涛教授的译诗，刷新了我对翻译诗歌的印象。首先，译文具有现代诗之美，表达流畅顺达而毫无拗口之感。诗集从开篇的"致敬，北京""好棒！好棒！"和"加勒比与全球"开始，就带给人朗朗上口、余韵无穷的感受。再者，译文译出了诗人保莉特·拉姆西教授诗歌创作的多样化品质。作为西印度群岛之国的牙买加独有的人物场景、热情豁达和坚毅的民族性格、美丽的风光景致、特有的地理历史背景等跃然纸上；加勒比人民寻求自我身份、超越民族主义和种族主义的人类关怀流露于诗人的笔尖。《牙买加诗歌集萃》中，"我学习跳舞""星果树和鳄梨树""回乡"等人物细腻的人物刻画，"老鼠夜出行""她恐惧""夸张的痛苦"强烈的内心感受描写，"诗歌比赛评委""诞生"折射的外在世界的矛盾和对加勒比黑人所处社会地位的强烈反应，"权利""假如"反映多元的自我意识并表现出在中美洲混杂的文化背景下的积极自我认知。最后，在这些诗歌译文中力透纸背、清晰可见的，是一位真正懂诗、具有诗人才情的编译者的匠心独运，是她与原作者相似的对人类共同命运的关怀和责任，以及自觉地对各民族文化的尊重和对跨文化交流事业的挚爱。也唯有如此才能让她对这外国诗歌具有透彻的理解并赋予贴切丰满的表达，才有她精雕细琢、下笔有神的翻译效果。

在国内现有拉美文学译介非常有限的背景下，《牙买加诗歌集萃》的编译选材优秀，作品清新精炼，翻译准确自然——这一体现民族"方言"的文学文化结晶，为人类看世界提供了新的视角——温情而幽默，诙谐而神秘，自信而达观，强烈地引发了读者的好奇心，堪称文学语言使用的典范。文中焕发活力光彩的诗行激荡着加勒比文学永恒跃动的节奏与韵律，使得读者可以尽情享受阅读、开阔视野，更可以开动脑筋，在全球语境下与诗歌展开文明互鉴的思想对话。在此期待侯涛教授今后有更多优秀的翻译成果问世，为读者带来与众不同的身心感受和文化体验。

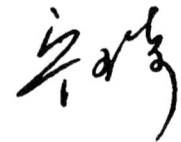

2019 年 11 月于北京大学

译 者 序

今年是太原理工大学和牙买加西印度大学莫纳分校（UWI at Mona）孔子学院建院十周年。在双方的共同努力下并受保莉特·拉姆西女士之邀（Paulette A.Ramsay 教授曾任牙买加西印度大学人文教育学院现代语言文学系主任，该大学在最新世界大学排名前5%，加勒比排名第一名），我将她的诗集《金星果树与鳄梨树》（Star Apple Blue and Avocado Green）中的诗歌选编并译成中文，籍此向国内外中文读者引介牙买加的语言、文学和文化，让广大读者领略牙买加诗歌文化一隅，感受其文学艺术之成就，借文学翻译增强中外文化交流和促进民心沟通，实为一件不可多得的幸事！

文学亘古永恒，而这本诗集的形式及内容给人的第一印象是新鲜。文学是人类创造性的表达，它帮助我们从表层经验走向对现实的深层认知。本诗集撷生活之精华，让普通人生活的点滴或思想瞬间的感受在作品中展开和升腾，感人至深、沁人心脾。围绕日常生活的话题——从牙买加原住民的衣、食、住、行，生长、婚嫁、教子直到年老失忆，从远行归来、人生起伏到世事沧桑，从村里、院里到世界之大，喜怒哀乐感情丰富，歌舞、鼓乐、绘画、文学刚柔并济。这些诗发端于当地独特的语言和文化的视角以及超脱的胸怀视野，成就了语言文学教授兼文学家保莉特·拉姆西成熟的学院派民歌诗人的创作风格，形成她独特的诗歌文学的主题和样式。

译者从一开始接触这些诗歌便被其中丰富多彩的艺术魅力所

感动，越读越是爱不释手，越译越感意犹未尽。这里的母爱、自然与童真，这里的责任、视野与理想，这里形神兼备的表达，既原生朴实又超世脱俗并且体现了后现代的诗风，有些更是蕴含着中牙文化交流的友好情谊。随着诗歌独特活泼的音乐跳动着的是作者的生活成长、日渐成熟的细心观察和乡思乡情，随着诗节流淌着的是一位睿智知识女性的敏锐热情与诗性洒脱，亦不乏对人类家园、共同命运和宏观世界社会历史发展、历史动向的思考。民谣式的风格中有中美洲原生说唱（hiphop）艺术的节奏、英语文学传统诗歌的精致思维以及非裔拉丁裔文学主题及背景的斑斓苍劲。总之，诗集饱含个性风格并充满文化特色。

要做好这项翻译，译者首先必须是一个了解源语语言文化的人，即了解牙买加的过去与现在、历史与风俗、社会和经济发展、人们的思想情感与哲学信仰，以及社会组织及文化成就。得益于2009年以来两校间不断开展、长期形成和逐步加深的教育文化交流活动，译者能够细致了解学习和深入体会感受目的语的语言文化。同时，译者面对翻译过程所必须面对的"矛盾之矛盾"问题，特别注意处理好诗歌形式与内容的相互关系，处理好诗歌翻译的共性和牙买加诗歌个性表现之间的关系，努力在牙买加诗歌语言文化与中文译入语文化之间实现贯通。譬如，直译的词句其顺序有时可能会影响阅读逻辑，必须经过调整，但调整之后还应该尽量保持原英文诗本身存在的特性。每及此时，译者首先顾及的是目标读者诗歌阅读的反映所必需要求的、为达到可读性和易读性的"真""善"和"美"；当形式与内容发生矛盾时，从不一概而论，而是分门别类——形式重要时形式第一，内容重要时内容第一。当两者矛盾时竭尽所能、力至均衡：做到作品在译入语读者那里朗朗上口并词句意义和意象意义准确，一切纯真"入文"

并体现文学美感。毕竟，原诗的诗体自成一派，诗体混用而自然由然、叙事与抒情一气呵成。在上述充分准备和思考的基础上，这次翻译工作整体较为顺利畅快，译得多时颇有豁然开朗之感。

文学文本阅读带给人们洞察人生和点亮生活的经验，如夏日清泉帮我们浇注心田，又似利斧神功帮我们凿劈认识的冰坚。在这一点上，拉姆西女士的诗集当之无愧——借助诗集的中译，使得我们虽拥有不同的肤色和讲着各自的语言，却能并肩思考人类共同命运的主题。欣赏这庄重轩逸、清丽活泼、热情幽默、奔放洒脱和来自遥远美丽的中美岛国"新民谣"式的诗歌，随着一首首小诗踏上牙买加生活的绮丽之旅，可感受诗歌文学（翻译）带给我们的文化交流的滋养！

经过几个月的打磨雕琢这本诗集即将问世，仅以此就教于广大专家学者和读者！

侯　涛
2019 年 11 月于太原理工大学

目 录

北京、世界 Beijing and Caribbean Global

Beijing Salute ·· 2

致敬，北京 ·· 3

Awesomesauce！ ·· 4

好棒！好棒！ ·· 5

Caribbean Global ·· 6

加勒比与全球 ·· 8

歌舞之灵 Dancing and Singing

I Learned to Dance ·· 11

我学习跳舞 ·· 13

The Reason She Sings ····································· 15

唱歌的理由 ·· 17

The Way She Was ··· 19

她原先的样子 ·· 21

自然灵感 Nature Metaphor

When the Yellow Pouis Bloom ···························· 24

当黄色地花菌盛开 ·· 26

Star Apple Blue and Avocado Green ····················· 28

金星果树与鳄梨树 ·· 30

1

Real Flowers ……… 32
真　花 ……… 34

母性、母爱 Mother's Love

Luna Mystery ……… 37
月球之谜 ……… 38
The Rats Come out at Nights ……… 39
老鼠夜出行 ……… 40
A Mother's Day Flight ……… 41
母亲节航班 ……… 42

勇敢女儿心 Brave Female

The Girl with the Big Heart ……… 44
她有一颗这样的心 ……… 45
(Re) making Self ……… 46
重建自我 ……… 47
Her Fear of Fear ……… 48
她怕恐惧 ……… 49
The First Mother ……… 50
第一位母亲 ……… 51
(Un) like Lot's Wife ……… 52
（不）似洛特的妻 ……… 53
Naissance ……… 54
诞　生 ……… 55

母性呵护 Mother Care

Mothers Make Magic ……… 57

创造奇迹的母亲 ………………………………………… 59
The Family Firm ………………………………………… 61
家庭医院 ……………………………………………… 65
Reflections on the Dirty Dishes in the Sink …………… 69
水池里的餐盘 ………………………………………… 71

向歧视说"不"Prejudice? No!

Human Rights …………………………………………… 74
权利 …………………………………………………… 75
(Un) wanted Poems ……………………………………… 76
诗歌比赛评委 ………………………………………… 77

生儿、教子 Birthing of Sons

Birthing of Sons ………………………………………… 79
生儿 …………………………………………………… 81
Last Will and Testament ………………………………… 83
嘱咐 …………………………………………………… 84

忘记与记忆 Forget Not

Forget Me Not …………………………………………… 86
勿忘 …………………………………………………… 87
Speaking in Halves ……………………………………… 88
言断续 ………………………………………………… 90

爱与失去 Loved and Lost

Going Back ……………………………………………… 93
回乡 …………………………………………………… 95

I Have Loved and Lost ………………………………… 97
我曾爱着和失去 ………………………………………… 99
Mourning a House ……………………………………… 101
失屋居 …………………………………………………… 103

说"夸张" Hyperbole

"Free Shampoo" ………………………………………… 106
"香波免费" ……………………………………………… 107
Grief in Hyperbole ……………………………………… 108
夸张的痛苦 ……………………………………………… 109
An Angry Woman Speaks to Her Body of Corpulence ……… 110
减肥 ……………………………………………………… 112

文学和文学家 Literature

One Hundred Years of Literary Indulgence …………… 115
一百年的文学浸润 ……………………………………… 116
Hypotheses ……………………………………………… 117
假如 ……………………………………………………… 120

村庄里不要害虫 Village Safe and Secure

I Remember ……………………………………………… 124
我记得 …………………………………………………… 127
Praying Mantis ………………………………………… 130
蝗虫在祷告 ……………………………………………… 131

北京、世界

Beijing and Caribbean Global

Beijing Salute

Me

black woman in China

I fell eyes x-ray me

Someone, curious, pulls my coarse hair, surprised

it does not separate from my scalp,

a woman, skeptical, touches my skin, surprised,

its black does not rub off,

and stain her hands

someone speaks to me

hello Africa

hello China, I say

we smile together,

we are people together,

me, Caribbean woman

she, Beijing woman.

致敬，北京

我
一个"非洲"女人在中国，
周围目光灼灼，
一只手好奇地揪我的发，
怎么，这头发未落下？
一只手惊战地触我的臂，
怎么，这墨色经得住蹭擦？
一个声音说话了，
"你好，非洲姐？"
我回答，
"你好，大妈！"
我们大家都笑了，
原来我们是一起的——
我，来自中美加勒比，
她，从小在北京长大。

Awesomesauce!

a Jamaican sprinter being chased
down the tracks in Beijing, London, Rio
a Jamaican hurdler taking gold
a Jamaican student who speaks
Chinese, French and Spanish

Awesomesauce!
Any Gabriel Garcia Marquez paragraph
a Barbadian eating Jamaican jerked pork
and showing it's the only real deal,
a Trinidadian jumping to Jamaican reggae
shouting that it is the music of all music
put calypso to shame
real reggae rhythms
Awesomesauce!

好棒！好棒！

在北京、伦敦、里约的赛场，
牙买加选手又冲上，
牙买加跨栏又填金！
牙买加学者用汉语、法语、西班牙语
在讲坛上讲话！

好棒！好棒！
加百利、加西亚、马尔克斯的文字啊，
巴巴多斯人欢迎的牙买加肉干，
赞赏！赞赏！
特立尼达人在雷鬼音乐中起舞，
这音乐超棒！
来点卡里帕索么？
不，不，雷鬼音乐高亢！
好棒！好棒！

Caribbean Global

"To be colonized is to be removed from history."
(Walter Rodney)

young St. Lucian artist
making deliberate strokes
paintbrush on white canvas
such panache,
the image of the Thames unfolds
revealing a poinciana, flamboyant,
on fire, on a tiny island
in the centre of the sleeping river,
the river flows undisturbed, around it
our young painter paints, with gusto

cool Jamaican bass guitarist
strumming his favourite reggae song
on a stage in Johannesburg
pom _pom _pom _podom _pom,
burum_ bum_ bum_ bum_ burum_ bum_ bum,
sounds of freedom

on the bass guitar
migration from Kingston, Georgetown, Bridgetown
to London, New York, Amsterdam, Brussels
journeying,
a reminder of home and self

gifted Grenadian student
in the library at the Ivy League University
in New England
writing new identities.

All over the world,
Caribbean people in action
decolonization in progress
Caribbean people
engaging oppositional politics
strumming the bass guitar
laughing othering in the face
writing freedom
strumming reggae songs
bodum, bom _bom _bom _bom _bom _bom !
borum, bom _bom _bom !
claiming space
bom—bom—bom—bom
borum—bom—bom !

加勒比与全球

"殖民化就是从历史上消失"
（瓦尔特 罗尼）

年轻的加勒比艺术家
大胆地画
油画笔刷在画布上，
那斑斓的画迹啊！
泰晤士河绵延长，
在其中的一块小岛上，
在沉沉的河正中央，
凤凰花儿正开放——红艳艳的火一样！
画面上的河静静流，
年轻画家在它周围画得酣畅！

在约堡古都的舞台上
酷酷的牙买加低音吉他手，
拍着鼓奏起雷鬼秀，
蹦 蹦 蹦，蹦蹬，蹦！
蹦蹬，蹦 蹦 蹦 蹦蹬 蹦 蹦！
低音吉他响——

自由的吼。
从金斯墩、乔治城、布里奇城,
走向伦敦、纽约、阿姆斯特朗和布鲁塞,
边走边唱
我爱自由、爱家乡!

格林纳达的学者新秀,
美国常青藤的
书桌后,
字迹铮铮书写着加勒比人新身份!
全世界呀,走一走,
加勒比人民在抖擞:
消除殖民主义,
加勒比人民
不要压迫
鼓舞着它的吉他手,
反对种族歧视
高声唱自由,
奏响雷鬼乐一首首
蹦蹬,蹦 蹦 蹦 蹦 蹦!
蹦蹬,蹦 蹦 蹦!
我们要自由。
蹦－蹦－蹦－蹦,
蹦蹬－蹦－蹦!

歌舞之灵

Dancing and Singing

I Learned to Dance

I learned to dance
to trample sorrow under feet

I learned to dance
so I could toss my head back
and move my shoulders and hips
to rhythms of freedom and joy

I learned to dance
to watch my body twirl and twist
with rhythmic ease

I learned to dance
so laughter would escape
from my mouth
as my body and soul
would glide upon the wings of rhythm

I learned to dance
so that my feet can join my hands and clap

together with the hills

leap, prance through the air

and I learned to dance, so you could see

that I love me, love to feel the cool green air

against my face

and that together me, my body and mind

have found rhythm and joy.

我学习跳舞

我学习跳舞，
学会将痛苦踩在脚下。

我学习跳舞，
头高扬、肩抖擞
嘴里咿咿呀，
和着那自由与欢快的诺维拉。

我学习跳舞，
让我的身体扭呀扭，
左三下、右三下。

我学习跳舞，
爽朗的笑声
发自肺腑，
我的身呀我的心
乘着翅膀轻盈盈。

我学习跳舞，

我跺脚呀我舞臂，
碰碰嚓嚓咔咔咔，
引得山峦跳动水腾跃。

我学习跳舞，
看到了吧，我呀我，
喜欢轻风拂我面，
我人我身与我心，
欢乐和愉悦！

The Reason She Sings

she can read her own letter now,
no more running to the fence
to beg Miss Mary or Mass Harold,
or the little ten year boy old across the road
to tell her what her sister
in America write to tell her

hallelujah !
she's discovered the gift of literacy
thanks to some people
who looked her in the eyes
told her to stop pretending
and taught her how to use
a, e, i, o, u, to make sounds
that make words and sentences
and made an honest woman of her

no more pretending
to be reading from the hymnal, on Sundays
no more twist up twist up mouth

to try to sing the same words
as Pastor, the choir and everybody else
every magazine in the doctor's office
every book on her own likkle bookshelf
bought for show, mere adornment
now screams at her
and she can tell what they all say

no more pretending her eye is dark
no more pretending she is hoarse
she can sing in her best soprano
the gift of words
the gift of the Word
the gift of reading, is the reason she sings,
hallelujah, hallelujah!

唱歌的理由

如今她能读信啦，
何屑跑过墙藩和篱笆
恳请玛丽或夏洛，
亦或走过马路去
向小小学童把话题提：
"喂，吾姊姊美国来信说啥呀？"

哈利路亚
有文化太好啦！
多亏好心的先生们
目光炯炯驱愚昧
令人真诚不佞虚，
教她说写
A、B、C……
教她造句美又美
知书达理她成人了！

不装啦，
以前礼拜假弥撒，
呜哑呜哑

"嗓子卡"
可如今，
办公桌上的册子，
自家架上书本本，
再也不是装饰品！
它们在"喊话"——
她知道它们说啥了！

不装眼睛看不清，
不装嗓门沙哑了！
她用动听的高音歌唱，
字的智灵，
字的智灵——
是令她歌唱的原因！

The Way She Was

rolled up tightly in a ball
cold and hard
like the metal on a well-built railway line,
daunting like Miss Clara James' cactus hedge,
afraid of her silhouette
afraid of her own reflection in the mirror
afraid of everyone, especially herself

then one day
the sun slid smoothly
from beneath thick cumulus clouds
in her head
the entire galaxy
all the purple blue waves of the Caribbean Sea and beyond
activated to the reggae beat
stifled in her head, through self-denying rites
and everyday rhythm became beautiful
and invigorating.

Now she smiles wistfully at butterflies

laughs at busy birds pecking at Julie mangoes

dances to Negro spirituals

hallelujah choruses

and conscious reggae rhythms

all the time

laughing with herself

laughing with the world,

making her own syncopated sounds

wondering why for so long

she refused to live.

她原先的样子

蜷又缩，

冰又硬，

轨道上头的铁一块

拒人远的"仙人篱"，

怕照镜子

怕见人，

亦怕"见"自己。

直到这样有一天，

阳光照亮天和地，

积云劈开混沌启，

银河漫天星耀熠，

加勒比海波碧涛倾，

雷鬼音乐的节奏里——

咦！咦！咦！ 原来全都怪自己！

生活原本这么美，

充满生机和活力！

笑看蝴蝶舞蹁跹，

喜逐小鸟啄芒果，

乐灵动、歌舞起，
哈利路亚歌声罢，
雷鬼音乐节奏疾——
一直地，
笑嘻嘻，
爱这世界
也爱自己，
呼啸声声震天外，
问问自己，
当初怎地不惬意？

自然灵感

Nature Metaphor

When the Yellow Pouis Bloom

the sun

can go to sleep,

rest,

in any corner

of the Caribbean

where yellow pouis

bloom

spread

their golden feathers

like a million

suns shattered

their golden rays

scattered

illuminating

every corner

brightening smiles

cooling hot water

evoking dreams

making eyes twinkle with glee

as each petal

glows

a golden yellow

shimmering

sparkling

like new gold.

当黄色地花菌盛开

太阳

可以入睡，

休憩

在黄色地花菌

盛开的

任意角落里，

伸展——

她们金色的毛蕊，

如百万个太阳，

铺撒

她们金色的光芒

遍染——

照耀

每一个地点，

启亮每一张笑脸，

点燃每一个梦想，

教每一双眼笑弯。

它的每一片花瓣

金黄

发散——

金子般的

闪亮。

Star Apple Blue and Avocado Green

our star apple tree is old and tired now
so many many years after my
great grandmother planted it
it now leans lazily yet gracefully
against the avocado tree that I planted
ten years ago
interestingly, they each carry stories
of two different generations
in a family that celebrates
our tropical trees with great spirit
my great grandmother loved the star apple's purple blue skin
and its succulent purple and white flesh
so delicately arranged in a wine coloured bowl
I planted my avocado for its smooth, waxy fruit
that my mother used to feed me
with hot slices of yellow heart roasted breadfruit
they seem to like each other's company
my avocado tree seems happy to
bear the weight of my great grandmother's
aged star apple tree with its purple green leaves

the star apple tree is happy to find

friendly support in a young strong trunk

in its last days

so reminiscent of the way great grandmother

loved the company of us young people

as we laughed and chattered around her

in her last days

our two trees seem to like

the cosiness of being snuggled against each other

listening to the soft whisper of their leaves

brushing against each other

in the quiet green breeze

sometimes I watch them with envy

I contemplate joining them

but then I wonder

who will I lean on

my avocado, or great grandmother's star apple?

for now, I'm content to just watch them

or close my eyes and imagine myself

sitting in the V where they meet

surrounded by star apple blue and avocado green

flowers and colours, my colours of life and joy.

金星果树与鳄梨树

金星果树老龙钟,
老姥姥种树
年代重重,
叶漫枝横匍匐立,
紧依着我种的
鳄梨"童"。
真有趣,两棵
有故事的
家庭树——
"热带树"的家风得继续:
老姥姥爱星果蓝紫色的皮,
也爱它白紫色的果肉瓤
叠摆在酒红色的果盘里;
我爱鳄梨的果肉腻腻,
母亲喂我吃满满的回忆,
配上猕猴桃"烤面包"……热抿更有趣!
两棵树儿相撑相予,
鳄梨小树最是欣喜,
是它撑住了金星果老树的翼,
那树翼叶子啊深幽幽的绿!

星果树啊心满意，

小树身挺立多么友谊，

在她年老的岁月里！

恰似那老嬷嬷们都喜欢

和青年人们在一起，一起——

叽叽喳喳又嬉戏，

相伴总是最惬意！

两棵树儿喜欣欣，

彼此依偎得温馨，

婆娑树叶沙沙地响

风中语儿轻盈盈——

她啊她啊相倾听。

我时看时想心妒忌，

好想置身她们里，

犹犹豫豫难决意，

依着哪个更相宜？

依那星果树？还是我的美食鳄梨？

——依不依，看看她们就心满意！

闭上眼，做个梦——

坐在两棵树的交叉里，

左金星果、右鳄梨，

花繁锦簇的生活——充满欢乐与爱意！

Real Flowers

when I was a little girl
I often picked golden marigolds
in my neighbour's wide open field
sometimes, early in the morning
when they were still wet with dew
sometimes, at midday
when they glowed in the golden sunlight
morning or midday
I tied them in little bundles
pretended I was a flower girl
and danced to the music in my head
holding them close to my face
pictured myself
carrying them to church
on Harvest Sunday

but always
I ended up
discarding them
with a secret wish

they were daffodils instead
the ones I saw in books
the ones I yearned for
and now
I deeply despise flowers
that only bloom in books.

真 花

童年时，
我常采撷金盏花，
在邻居家宽阔的田地；
有时就在清晨里，
金盏花儿晨露滴；
有时恰在正午，
金盏花朵金熠熠。
不论早晨或正午，
金盏花呀扎小朵，
自己就是那卖花女，
——心中奏乐把舞起！
金盏花呀贴贴面，
想自己，
在丰收时节的周末，
握着它走进那圣殿……

可总是，
到后来，
我丢弃了金盏花，
暗期许：

金盏花变成水仙花，

书里讲起的水仙花，

我那渴望的水仙花……

到如今，

我蔑视花

——书里盛开的艳俗的花。

母性、母爱

Mother's Love

Luna Mystery

nobody ever spoke

the truth

there is a woman in the moon

una mujer en la luna

just a man and his dog

they always say,

just imagine

the world being like

that moon.

月球之谜

没有人讲出
真实话,
月亮上有个女人,
有个女人在月亮上。
——月亮上只有个男人和一只狗,
他们总在说。
可试想,
这世界如果真变成
那个月亮……

The Rats Come out at Nights

right after she puts her children to bed
they move stealthily, like cowardly thieves
and feverishly nibble at the dried bread
she feeds her children for supper
she will use her bare hands
to smother the life
out of them
if she but catches them
trying to steal to live, spread diseases
and disturb her children's sleep
or even the siesta of her indolent cats.

老鼠夜出行

趁母方哄儿入睡,
贼鼠头,怯怯地,
狂啃狂食干面包,
——吾儿餐饭吃啥哩?
动手吧,
逮老鼠!
掐死它——
要是逮住就好了!
鼠偷鼠窃鼠传疫,
打扰吾儿少休息,
猫母全都不得憩!

A Mother's Day Flight

it was a reunion
a Mother's Day plan
to meet estranged children
cover the wound with new cloth
stitch the patches with new thread
the anticipation and doubt
the happiness and fear
the longing and hope
the questions without answers
the certainty and uncertainty
too much for a heart
broken many times
by disappointment
the mother collapses on the tarmac
at Vere Bird International Airport
like an over-moist paper bag
and dies
while a repentant son
waits in the arrival lounge
pensively and patiently...

母亲节航班

母亲节
来团聚
看看久已疏远的儿——
新衣可能抚慰旧痕?
密缝定能补离伤!
希望又迟疑,
欣喜又惆怅——
母亲日思昼想儿,
此情终得报偿?
盼之切、
失之痛,
娘心情
不堪忍——
纸裱的衣袋淋湿了塌,
娘亲就倒在了机翼旁——
在维尔伯机场的草坪上
嗟乎哀!
伤心的儿子啊,
候机室的座椅上,
心情空悲伤……

勇敢女儿心
Brave Female

The Girl with the Big Heart

hers is a heart

not unused to being broken apart

by many a dart

even from the arrows

of treacherous lovers

not one to take cover, or cower

she takes the blows

one by one,

and quietly keeps count

for she knows, without doubt

that time and pain

will both bring gain

mend her heart

set her apart

from those who are meek

faint-hearted and weak.

她有一颗这样的心

百般磨难终不碎,
任箭穿心,
真情背,
不防御、不撤离、不回避,
箭如发,
矢中的,
她默默数着一又一
她心中,最坚信:
要待时光流逝苦熬去,
收获渐来抚慰心!
只因为——
她不惧,
她不假,
心坚毅!

(Re)making Self

no stones

no blocks

no steel

just woman will

spiritual reconnection

with Mother earth

communion with the Almighty.

inevitable in this mess

reflection, on how they define me

rejection, of how they define me

self-rewrite

remade woman of pride

moving my unaggressive face

into everybody's space

silencing the myth-makers.

重建自我

不用砖，

不用石，

不用钢，

只用女性毅力，

用她来自母亲大地之精神，

用来自大自然之灵感。

反思，他们怎样定义了我？

反思，他们的定义我怎样重写？

重建！自信的女性！

我无辜的脸看向每个人的思维空间——

让神话的编造者哑口无言！

Her Fear of Fear

She fears fear.

she hates the way

it curls up inside of her

and squashes

her very core

she dreads fear

deeply...

她怕恐惧

她怕恐惧，
　她恨
恐惧蜷缩在心底，
扰乱她的人生梦；
　她恐惧恐惧——
　　她深深恐惧
　　　那恐惧。

The First Mother

the first mother did not prick
her fingers picking
red roses for her children or her man
she just ate
the wrong fruit
they say that's how
she hurt herself

the first mother was denied
the chance to mother
it was her fault you say
that's how she robbed herself
and lived the life
of a dried up peach
trying to see life and joy
beyond the restless purple—blue waves
where heaven and earth meet.

第一位母亲

第一位母亲没有
采撷
给孩子或给爱人的玫瑰
她只食了
不该吃的果实
众惊愕——
她从此自欺
熬度
残岁,
隔了蓝色汹涌的海浪
——望人世

(Un)like Lot's Wife

like Lot's wife
I turned into a pillar of salt
understood the error
of looking back;
(un)like Lot's wife
I melted slowly
and survived
on the salt
of my molten tears.

（不）似洛特的妻

我似洛特的妻
　　变盐柱，
　　明知这是，
　　回望的错。
我又不似洛特的妻
　　我融化，
　　又重生；
　　盐柱上，
　　我泪凄凄。

Naissance

of your indifference
I do not know...
of your hatred
I cannot rationalize
naissance
of your self-centredness
I will never fathom
or your deeply entrenched sexism
I will never accept.

诞　生

你冷漠，

我不晓，

你憎恶，

我莫知，

诞生……

你自私，

我不睬，

你若不尊重女性，

——吾将永不受！

母性呵护

Mother Care

Mothers Make Magic

(For mothers everywhere)

they create magic
mothers do
everyday
they stretch time like endless
elastic ropes
that children swing on
to the moon and back
mothers
make tuneful onomatopoeia
and put the night on hold,
they keep the day running
as their sons float their kites
on the wind,
games must be played,
bodies fed,
fantasies spun
with the thread
of magical words,

songs must be sung,

the stars repainted in the sky

everyone must go to the moon

and back

as mothers make magic.

创造奇迹的母亲

（致所有的妈妈们）

母亲的劳动
每日
创造奇迹。
她们总是抽出时间，
似橡皮筋，
孩子们悠的橡皮筋，
悠起来呀又落下。
妈妈的哼唱多悠扬，
每个傍晚听着多欢畅。
白日里也少不了——
男孩们乘风
放风筝；
游戏罢，
美味享，
妈妈的声音
多奇妙，
把一连串的故事讲，
歌声还飞扬！

今夜里天上星闪亮，
你遐想，我遐想
妈妈们啊在哼唱！

The Family Firm

my two grandmothers formed

a two—woman firm

and together

they cured all forms of illnesses

afflictions and maladies

of my cousins, siblings

aunts, uncles

the whole village

every bruised knee

running nose

running belly

loss of appetite

sore gum

necessitated a trip

to one or the other

for one had the cure

for blood and skin problems,

the other the cure

for eyes, nose and throat

belly and lung problems

their instruments were their eyes
sharp, piercing, probing.
they spun us in all directions
studied our eyes
pressed our ear lobes
poked us in the ribs and cheeks
made their diagnosis
and gave us medicine
from their medicine chests

cool soothing
sticky ointments
green and brown liquids
all created from plants
they pulled from their gardens,
a serious illness
could mean
ginger and lemon grass
or guinea hen weed, cerasee
or tamarind leaves
arrow root or aniseed tea

they had a bush or grass

or leaf for every illness
and when we swallowed
bitter aqueous substances
we doubted not once
that our bellies
would soon feel good
when we gritted our teeth
as stinging crushed leaves
or peppery powder was
spread on our sores
we believed
we would be healed
soon, soon
and when we could run
skip and play hopscotch
we knew that they
had healed us with
magical medicines
from their gardens,

and we believed
that one day we could
be just as they were
doctors with healing potions
but we never learnt their secrets

never had their touch

never studied their plants

and so we tell the story

that they were the

best doctors we

ever knew.

家庭医院

我的两位祖母创立
姐妹医院，
她们一起
治愈这病那瘟，
千疾百患，
医了我的兄妹表亲，
姨舅叔伯，
和全村的人——

每有青淤、
鼻塞、
腹泻、
胃、
齿痛，
或
快去看见
姐姐和妹妹！
姐姐会瞧
血色和皮肤、
妹妹能看

眼鼻喉弊、

腹脾和肺疾。

她们的仪器似慧眼，

看准、查清、诊得全：

转眼睛，

压耳朵，

这边看完转那边，

脸颊身体打量遍！

确了诊，

再付药，

药箱打开一串串：

霜爽粉，

油膏膏，

绿色红色的药水水，

全都来自树秧秧，

花园里的禾秧秧！

头疾脑热病倒了，

生姜、柠檬

来治疗，

几内亚鸡草、葫芦瓜，

葛根、罗望子煮八角。

百种疾病

百草治，

咽下

苦汁

放心了——

腹痛

这就好！

磕磕牙，

嚼碎叶，

胡椒粉撒进

牙槽槽——

不怀疑、莫多虑，

我这就会健康的！

我能跑了！

我能跳了！

我的心啊它知道

是它们

把我治疗好：

奶奶们花园里的

仙人草！

我常想

等长大

也弄医药

行医治病那叫个好！

可不知其"法"，

不得其妙，

更不解她们的草药，

只好讲个故事罢——
她们是我见过
最好的
医和匠!

Reflections on the Dirty Dishes in the Sink

(For Heather Bowie)

I do not own

the dirty dishes in the sink

they really do not belong to me

they certainly are not part

of some special collection

of dirty things that I own.

I sometimes explain

to myself, to the air

to those who listen to me

that of the ten dirty cups in the sink

my DNA can be found on one

and on one fork, one knife

and perhaps a tiny teaspoon,

do not expect then to be praised

each time you wash the dishes

and please, I beg of you

do not wash the dishes

as a special favour to me

do not think of me

as the lucky beneficiary

of your thoughtfulness

just do the dishes because you care

about keeping the world

free from your germs.

Or perhaps, because you need them clean

for the next time you need to eat or drink.

水池里的餐盘

（写给海瑟·堡卫）

池中脏盘
非我有，
我即非主人；
吾故喜古物
彼亦非吾
收集品。

日里吾常
慰自己、慰无形，
慰于彼——
池中餐盘有十只
只有一只是我的，
一副刀叉
一把勺，
君若替吾将餐具洗，
一次一赞是不可能的；
行行好、求求你，
"特意"地清洗

不需要!

不感恩,

无谢意,

——不用"专为"我考虑!

盘碟脏了君清洗,

细菌污物

都离去;

或者说,卫生重要,

每用每洗洁净餐具!

向歧视说"不"

Prejudice? No！

Human Rights

(for all people)

right to say so and so,
we like to say,
right to do so and apparently so,
some people fight,
to show their rights
are the only rights
that matter
some people fight
to show the rest of us
we should not speak
we should not do
or even be.

权利

欲言，
则言；
欲为，
则为。
有人在战斗，
因他们的权利
是唯一
重要的权利；
有人在战斗，
示意我们"之类"，
——我们不应该说
——我们不应该做
——不应该存在。

(Un)wanted Poems

During the reading
I avoided their eyes
after the reading
I avoided their eyes
the poets before me
made them laugh,
now they smiled at me feebly
some seeming to see me
as a mere figure of fun.

Someone muttered garbled words
something about nation language
and yet another mumbled
something about poems
that were too staid and puny
needing a little carnivalesque
and yet another suggested
a little reggae riddim
woulda good yes
I smiled feebly at them
and avoided their probing eyes.

诗歌比赛评委

我读我的，
不看他们的眼，
我读完一首，
仍不看他们的眼，
我面前的这群人，
我让他们见笑了——
他们狡黠地笑，
藐视
我这"可笑的家伙"！

有人吱吱又呜呜，
"民族……民族……这是民族语"，
有人欲言却又止，
说这诗，
貌似正经又羸弱，
需要加入狂欢化——
人群里这下炸了锅，
"来点雷鬼，哈哈……很不错！"
我只轻轻一笑，
任你目光叱喝——
试问你们还知道什么？

生儿、教子

Birthing of Sons

Birthing of Sons

Men, all two
they leave a mother's day card
hidden in my handbag
I read it and smile
reminisce on fourteen hours of travail
to bring forth the first to light
and the voice of
the anaesthetist counting to ten
while I mutter
yeah though I walk
through the valley of the shadow of death
before they plucked
the second one
from my womb
flesh of my flesh
one born in Spring at dawn
the other in the mid-morning Summer's sun.

Strong black men
they will help their country

keep its pride

and take women

through the rites

of bringing men and women

into the world.

生儿

儿子,两个
是他们把母亲节卡片
放进了我的挎包
卡读罢,我笑了——
十几个小时苦熬过,
大儿到了人世间。
麻醉师数数,
我说"好",
此生横跨生死谷,
二儿才
从我的体内
降生下。
我的骨啊我的肉
一个诞在春晓前,
一个生于夏晨后。

黑小伙,体格壮,
国家命运
肩上扛,
也将携着心上人

一同走过婚礼路，
　　将男儿、女儿
　　带到这世界上！

Last Will and Testament

(for Marc and Zac)

to my two sons, I bequeath you
my words,
firm and pointed
many edged swords
infused with the Word
the spring of all gifts, incomparable,
you will
carry them in your heads
and in your hearts
they'll keep you new every morning
grounded deep
in light and truth.

嘱咐

（写给马克和赛克）

对我的两个儿子，我给予你们
　　我的话
　　　凝重、洗练，
　　　　如利剑，
　　　话里充盈
　　泉思睿智，
　　　你们将
　　　　心领
　　　　　神会
　　　晨沐弥新，
　　　　伫立
　　光与真理中。

忘记与记忆

Forget Not

Forget Me Not

(For daughters and sons...from any parent)

When I begin to forget
who I am
who you are
where I'm from,
where you are from
will you be there
to remind me?

And when you help me to remember
will you also remember
for my sake, and yours
our best kept secrets and fondest memories,
lend will you remember to
smile at the sea for me

勿忘

（一位老人致年轻人）

当我渐渐地忘记，
　我是谁，
　你又是谁，
　我的过去，
　你的过去，
你可能帮我来回忆？

当你帮我来回忆，
你可能帮我记得起，
——为了我、也为了你，
心底的秘密和惬意，
你可也会记得起——
替我微笑看大海……

Speaking in Halves

have you ever noticed how these days
I speak in halves
half a sentence
half a word
half a thought
even half a syllable

it's my mind you see,
beginning to remember in halves
forgetting in halves
I dread the thought
of remembering nothing,
forgetting all

If you listen
you will realise
I remember only half
your name
you'd be surprised
If I told you

I remember only half your face
I call my child by half his name
you, Em, I say for Emanuel
you, Pe, I say for what they
say is Petunia

And now I'm beginning
to wonder
how much of me
do I really remember
all, or half
and if only a half,
which half...

言断续

你可留意近些天,
我吞吞吐吐言断续,
半句话,
半个词,
半点子,
半个音……

我这脑子啊,
开始记半星儿,
忘半星儿,
可怕吗?
记不得
忘干了……

听听吧、看看吧:
却原来,
我只记得
你半个名,
咋搞的?
我只记得你半张脸,

我唤孩子半个名，
艾玛努尔唤"艾玛"，
佩图尼尔叫做"佩"。

终有一天我恐怕，
自己连自己也记不起，
　记得多少——
　也"一半"？
　　真一半，
　　　哪一半？

爱与失去

Loved and Lost

Going Back

when I returned
to the place I had carried in my head
for such a long time
I squeezed myself
into the tiny space
chagrined...
somehow I remembered it
differently...

when I was a little girl
it was a vast playing field
now the bench
can hardly hold my books

when I returned
to the place I had carried in my head
for such a long time
complacent dust stirred, tickled my nostrils
cottony cobwebs clouded my vision
I struggled to see in the dark

somehow

I remembered it

differently

when I was a little girl

it was a bright sunny garden

now the rays of the sun

barely penetrate the cloud of gloom

hanging over it

such a funny thing it is...

remembering.

回乡

我回到阔别许久、记忆深处的地方，
心中不解又惆怅，
逼自己进入这窄巷，
怎么，我记得它不是这个样——
从前少小年幼时
这是多么大的游乐场！
可如今的这条椅，
书本放上都够呛。

回到那
很久前
记忆深处的地方，
浮尘荡起来呛鼻腔呛，
蜘蛛网锁住视线前方，
我举目将暗处细打量，
怎么，
记得它不是这个样！

那时的我还年幼，
花园里光彩四处流淌，

可如今这太阳光亮，
　只微微透过厚的云
洒在花园的顶上……
　　记忆啊，
你怎么会是这个样？

I Have Loved and Lost

many things,

in many different ways,

my grandmother's antiquated wooden house

eaten to the ground by pitiless termites,

my innocent village

over-run by uninvited strangers

with no love in their hearts, no love

for our breadfruit trees

our star-apples and hog plums,

our unsophisticated old people, simple and sincere

our parochial young children.

I've loved and lost

a house that still carries the echo of my voice

decorated with the delicate strings of my heart

I've loved and lost

my favourite avocado green shoes, pliable leather

that made me sympathise

with the bovine that surrendered its life

just for my feet

carried off by yesterday's flood waters
that sucked them from my soles
clapping as they skipped away with them, thieving waters.
It's a truth most people now believe
that one day they will lose everything
especially what they love most
while the world will continue
to breathe, live and laugh.

我曾爱着和失去

我曾爱着和失去，
许多样的好东西，
或者这样或那样！
难忘祖母的老木屋，
狠心的白蚁吞噬倾；
温馨安宁的村乡故里，
不容分说就拆平去！
——心中无爱啊，心不爱：
高大可敬的面包树，
葱郁的星果和霍李，
温存善良的老人啊、淳朴天真的
童男女！

我曾爱着和失去，
回声飘荡的大房子，
墙上有可爱的花装饰；
我曾爱着和失去，
可爱的牛果绿鞋子——皮软软，
那乖水牛，
呵护着我的脚踝踝——

大水中她们被冲走，
从我的脚丫下猛冲走，
啪啪踏踏地被携走，被那山洪冲走了！
难怪乎，众人言：
爱与守，终别弃，
越是爱，越分离；
世界啊，在继续——
真情可足惜？

Mourning a House

the loss of a house
one you've lived in all your life
is like a miscarriage
losing the child
you have been growing inside of you
for months

you feel the fingers of pain twist deep
inside your abdomen
you feel the sharp teeth
of disappointment and loss
you feel the nausea
caused by interminable regret, remorse
for long-term and short-term dreams unrealized

you remember the corner of the garden
where you planned to grow some red roses, one day
how you planned to paint the kitchen
in your favourite calypso yellow, and how
you meant to trim the mango tree

that shades the back verandah

you flinch from the guilt of abandoning this house
as you would each time
the image of your still-born child
would come to mind...
eventually, you can only grieve in silence

no-one wants to know your grief or pain
so you just keep on smiling at the sea.

失屋居

失屋居，
失去世代居住的老屋居，
正如
失去胎儿
那孕育数月
腹中的儿——

深深的痛啊
在腹低，
失魂落魄在
咬自己，
悔恨拂不去，
心痛至极！
朝思暮想啊，你怎说去就去？

记得在花园的角落里，
玫瑰花刚刚栽进了地，趁须臾
粉刷厨房的墙壁
用上最心爱的亮黄油漆。这——
就来裁剪芒果树翼，

凉亭遮住些好休息——

失家的苦闷欲脱去，
　　却每每
　　忆"儿"
　　在梦里……
　　　空抽泣

痛苦惆怅向谁倾诉？
看大海——它的碧波闪动亮盈盈……

说"夸张"

Hyperbole

"Free Shampoo"

the neon sign stressed
"Free shampoo for every weave"
imagine...
they would punish me
for wearing my own hair
make me pay for my own shampoo...

but, if I bought the hair of a monk
or a cadaver in India or Brazil
and glued it to my scalp
they would reward me,
I could get my hair washed
with essence of coconut oil,
lime leaf and mint
without paying a cent
imagine that...

"香波免费"

霓虹灯箱闪,
"美发香波免费送",
谁曾信……
我这就要被人坑——
辨个喜欢的发型,
自卖洗发精……

花钱买个假发顶,
哪里弄来的不要紧,
黏到头上,
有好事——
洗头请用
椰油精
薄荷橙精,
分文不取,
谁敢信……

Grief in Hyperbole

when Suzie got news
of Johnny's death
her bones turned to water,
she fell to the ground
and wept blood
that clotted as it fell to the ground
like huge balls of stone

such grief
Miss Jane
had never seen
in her century-long life
and she wept torments of water
for Suzie
for she believed in
grieving for the living

夸张的痛苦

当苏西听说
约翰的死,
她浑身骨散,
瘫下去,
呜呜呜,
血块落地,
犹如巨石滚在地!

百龄
简奶奶
如此的大悲
一生未遇,
简老顿时假嚎啕,
——她悼苏西
上演一曲
活人"祭"。

An Angry Woman Speaks to Her Body of Corpulence

so you have I notice   I can hardly not notice,
resolved to defy me   it's truly outrageous,
not to yield one ounce
of obdurate lard   I am amazed at this,
despite days of flagellation
months of climbing
treacherous mountains
you insist on hanging on   as unbelievable as it is,
to every dangling part
every tightly rolled
ball of lard

forget appeals to pathos
forget appeals to logic
you remain
an artistic menace

but be warned that today   I jump and tuist
without success
the size six purple-blue frock mocks me still

but I promise you
you will shrink
to near obscurity...
one day.

it is a sure threat,
I can visualise it,

减肥

这下让我看清了，我也无法看不清，
你铁心和我过不去。这让人也太生气，
一盎司也不丢弃，
你顽固不化的大油腻，吓人哩！

日复日的鞭子勒，
月复月地练爬山。
艰难险峻的高山，
你紧贴在那——不可思议，
摇摇晃晃的肚囊底，
圆圆滚滚的肉袋体！

没同情，
不讲理，
你丑呆呆地不知趣，
今儿可是警告你！我使劲跳，我大力甩，
可你还是留在原地。
大号的紫裙都笑我傻！
我要郑重告诫你，虽是怨恨地，
有一天，

你是会要变小的,在我的梦幻里,

　　小得无踪迹!

文学和文学家

Literature

One Hundred Years of Literary Indulgence

(For Gabriel Garcia Marquez)

another hundred years,
we who come after
those who came before
and those who follow the ones
after us
and those after them
will read your stories
search the pages
criss-cross of endless words
and short sentences
labyrinth of complex images
painted with your multi-coloured words
for a hundred years and more...

一百年的文学浸润

（致加百利　加西亚　马尔克斯）

我们这一代，
继我们上一代，
再过一百年，
我们之后的之后
后代的后代，
都将拜读你的作品，
一页一页翻阅
字里行间，
读你浓墨重彩的语言
描绘的神秘而富有哲思的图景，
一百年又一百年……

Hypotheses

If I lived in a far-away place
they would send a supersonic jet for me
roll out a red and velvet carpet
and enclose me in a circle of love
they would touch my face
tell me my skin is soft
mop the sticky sweat from my brow
with a never before used linen handkerchief
crown me with the colour of orange marigolds
present me with native tokens
and say here
take this
this is the word of our mouths
flesh of our flesh
make it yours
you are part of us now
you are us

write
we will read

speak

we will listen

cover our rocky paths with words

like soft hibiscus petals

paint pictures of beauty

never before imagined

speak any truths you know

if I lived here and left

and came again

they would touch my face

tell me it is beautiful, soft

unusual, striking

they would say speak

inscribe your words

on our hearts and faces

take our words

and transform them with your magical touch

ones you discovered in faraway lands

if I came from far away

they would take me

to the squares, the plazas

where sophisticated old ladies

sit and sip red and white teas

they would take me to the bar
where young intellectuals
sit and debate the politics of inclusiveness
they would at last take me
and say they truly know me.

if I came from far away
or left and returned
they would kiss my ring
read my words
and confess
their undying love.

假如

假如我住在大老远，
超音机会派来接我返，
铺上紫色大红地毯，
众星捧月般将我揽，
赞我的肌肤有多软，
芬芳洁净的香手帕，
揩去我额头的粘汗，
赠予我金簪花美花环，
给予我当地的礼赞，
快请收下这所有的——
"您"就是"我"，
我们从此就是"咱"！

您的文字
我们捧读，
您的言语
我们恭听！

开启尊口言几句，
芙蓉花瓣落满地；

画张画儿美不美,
千年万载数第一;
您的话全都是真理!

寄寓他乡
回家返,
碰面就有人向我喊:
锦衣玉体换了新颜,
口里还把金丹含!
说要我讲上一番话,
他们定要字字
记心坎——
"土蛮话"请我
来改善,
盼我点石成金把"魔法棒"闪!

我若游远回家返,
常被迎到
广厦盛宴,
腐腐朽朽的贵太太,
高台座上正抿茶叶;
我也常被引到吧台边——
年轻俊逸的知识人,
公平正义的话题谈,
是他们真正了解我!——

我心终被他们"沦陷"。

  我寄宿他乡
  回家园，
  他们敬我
   读我，
    说
  爱我永远！

村庄里不要害虫

Village Safe and Secure

I Remember

I remember when
my village was the Garden of Eden
we romped and rolled around in the big den
we were all owners
or rather the grown-ups were
we children reaped,
"You can pick anything
except mi mint bush,"
Miss Millie would shout

We picked red, yellow, purple blossoms
from her shoe black bush
marigold and lady slippers
adorned our hair with little bouquets
plucked rose petals and sprinkled them
and frightened shame-o-I-ladies,
along our paths.

I remember when
our village was an orchard

we were all planters

or rather, the men and women tended

watered, manure, we children reaped

ate the first, second and third fruits

we bit into their firm skins

succulents, drupes, berries

juice oozing through our fingers

down to our elbows.

"Pick anything except mi Julie Mango"

Miss Sybil would say

we remembered our manners

thanked her and moved on

to Miss Dill's Star Apples

and I remember when my village

was a playing field

safe, secure, sheltered from evil

we were all innocent

oblivious to harm, and suffering

we all played and the grownups, cheered

we never saw him

lurking in the background

the monster that would change our village

rob us of its Arcadian charm
"careful how you walk through de ball ground,"
Miss Dasa shouts now
as we sit and remember
our village
the way it used to be.

我记得

我记得，
村子是个大花园，
猫猫洞里我们无忧地玩，
村子就是我们的，
——是大人们的，
我们小孩把收割管——
"想摘什么摘什么，
除过我那绿薄荷"，
米粒小姐这样言。

我们摘红的、黄的、紫色的，
就从她家的灌木前，
金盏花和兜兰华
华冠扮美额头簪，
玫瑰花瓣儿殷殷红，
扑散开吓坏太奶奶，
一路上真高兴！

我记得
村子是个大果园，

各种果树种植欢，
——是大人们种，
他们勤浇水、勤施肥，小孩来收获，
第一、第二、第三个果，
脆果皮牙齿就咬进了，
核果、肉果或浆果，
汁液淌在手指间，
流得一胳膊粘！

"摘果吧！别摘我的朱莉芒"
西伯尔小姐这么说，
小伙伴们相配合，
听了谢过就不见了——
跑向迪尔小姐家金星果。

我也记得那时我们村
是一大片的游乐园，
恬静安宁的好家园，
男孩女孩无牵念，
不怕冒险，
尽情地玩，
大人们在旁笑开颜。

从来没有听说过，
在那角落里的树丛间，

藏着的破坏村子的大魔煞,

宁静平和不见了,

迪赛小姐紧着喊,

"小心啊!穿过球场别缺心眼!"

坐稳稳、仔细想——

我们村

原来多安全……

Praying Mantis

praying Mantis

camouflaging himself

in my exuberant hibiscus hedge

pretending to pray

but waiting to pounce

on an innocent prey

not at all like a prayer warrior

even if a prayer warrior

sometimes prays for deadly stings

and bites

upon any

who would prey on the weak

the helpless and the praying

praying mantis

devourer of careless vreatures

hardly ever pernickety

a silent killer

pretending to pray

in my bountiful hibiscus hedge.

螳虫在祷告

螳虫在祷告,
它埋伏
在郁郁葱葱的木槿花丛,
假惺惺地在祷告,
却蠢蠢欲动
预备扑向一旁自由自在的小昆虫!

根本不像圣斗士
没有谁蛰痛他不翻脸,
他尖牙利齿
专门咬
那欺凌无辜的
大坏蛋,
——让弱小者摆脱危险!

螳虫在祷告,
这乱吞无辜
铁石心肠的
暗杀手,
在郁郁葱葱的木槿花上
假惺惺地装作在祷告……